ISBN 978-0-282-20891-2
PIBN 10844505

1 MONTH OF FREE READING

at

www.ForgottenBooks.com

By purchasing this book you are eligible for one month membership to ForgottenBooks.com, giving you unlimited access to our entire collection of over 1,000,000 titles via our web site and mobile apps.

To claim your free month visit:

www.forgottenbooks.com/free844505

English
Français
Deutsche
Italiano
Español
Português

www.forgottenbooks.com

Mythology Photography **Fiction**
Fishing Christianity **Art** Cooking
Essays Buddhism Freemasonry
Medicine **Biology** Music **Ancient**
Egypt Evolution Carpentry Physics
Dance Geology **Mathematics** Fitness
Shakespeare **Folklore** Yoga Marketing
Confidence Immortality Biographies
Poetry **Psychology** Witchcraft
Electronics Chemistry History **Law**
Accounting **Philosophy** Anthropology
Alchemy Drama Quantum Mechanics
Atheism Sexual Health **Ancient History**
Entrepreneurship Languages Sport
Paleontology Needlework Islam
Metaphysics Investment Archaeology
Parenting Statistics Criminology
Motivational

A FIG

FOR FORTUNE.

BY

ANTHONIE COPLEY.

PRINTED FOR THE SPENSER SOCIETY.

1883.

QVM MORTVI VERSOR

PRINTED BY CHARLES E. SIMMS,
MANCHESTER.

A FIG FOR
Fortune.

Recta Securus.

A. C.

LONDON
Printed by Richard Iohnes for C. A. 1596.

To the Right Honourable

Anthonie Browne, L. Vicompt Mont-ague, euerla-
fting glorie to his vertues.

FLie vale-bred Mufe to heauen-high *Mont-ague*
Honoring thy playneffe with fo quaint afpire :
It is a haggard Hawke that neuer knew
The Fawlkoners fift ; It is a drowfie fire
That yeelds nor flame nor fume ; It is an idle voyce
That nere was hard to tune nor found, nor note nor
Great *Mont-ague* ; thrife great in Vertues glorie   (noife.
And therfore dulie great in my affections,
Whom not a Pick-thanke fpirit of flatterie
But well aduifed zeale to your perfections
Mooues to inftile you fo : Though likewife fo you be
In the fublimitie of your blood and Vicomptie.
Daigne in your grace the fpirit of a man
Difaftred for vertue ; if at leaft it be
Difafter to be winnowed out Fortunes Fan
Into the Fan of Grace and Sionrie
Wherin repurify'd to Gods eternall glorie
The Deuill rues in man old *Adams* injurie.
Though meane and merit-leffe the Mufe may feeme
To your aduice ; as not from *Helicon,*
Yet well I hope the matter will redeeme
That frail default, as fpirited from *Sion* :
If *Sions* holie name be gracious to your eare
Hold it in gree ; elfe for the zeale to you I beare,
At leaft your happie Names faire liuerie let it weare.

Your Lordfh. humblie at commandement.

Anthonie Copley.

The Argument to
the Reader.

*A*N Elizian *out-caſt of Fortune, ranging on his Iade* Melancholie *through the Deſert of his affliction, in hope to find out ſome where either eaſe or end of the ſame, hapneth firſt upon* Ca-toes *ghoſt a ſpirit of Diſpair & ſelf-miſdoom which perſwades him to kill himſelfe: But, for ſhe ended her Oratory with a Sulphur vaniſh frō out his ſight, he miſdoubted both her and her tale. Then poſting onward through the reſidue of the night; he next chanceth on the ſpirit of* Re-uenge: *She perſwades him blood and treacherie againſt all his enemies, as th'onlie means to remount to priſtin bleſſe in deſpight of Fortune: But ſhe likewiſe manifeſting in the end the treaſon of her tale by a ſudden whip away from his eye at the ſight of break of day in the Eaſt, left him alſo conceipted of her daunger. Thirdly, rapt from off his* Melancholie *(which now began to faint vnder him at the light of a new day of Grace) he was ſuddenlie mounted vpon the Steed of* Good Deſire, *and by him brought to Mount-*Sion *the Temple of Peace; where by* Cate-chryſius *an Hermit (who greatlie woondred to ſee a diſtreſsed* Elizian *in thoſe partes vnder ſo happie daies of* Eliza*) he was by him in the houſe of* Deuotion *catechized, and there alſo celeſtially arm'd by an Angell, and within a while after in-denized by the high Sacrificator a Champion of that* Temple *againſt the inſults of Fortune; whom I haue titled by the name of* Dobleſſa

The Argument.

in re∫pect of the double danger both of her luring and lowring inconstancie: She, whiles the Sionites were all in peacefull adoration of Almightie God in the Temple, came with her Babelonian-rout to a∫sault the place, but was eft∫oons by the valure of tho∫e Templers ∫hamefullie repul∫ed: Fea∫t and thankes was made to God therfore throughout all the Region; in which∫olemnitie the Grace of God houering ouer the multitude in the Proce∫sion-time like a virgin attended vpon with all the Court of heauen, ∫howr'd downe Ro∫es among∫t them, leauing them there a ∫cambling for the ∫ame. The Elizian *was one that ∫cambled his lap-full among the re∫t: and for he thought it was his ∫oueraigne Ladie* Eliza, *and tho∫e* Ro∫es *hers, he was ∫uddenly in ioy therof rapt home againe to* Elizium.

Faultes e∫caped in printing.

Pag 5. Lin 18 It ∫huts it ∫elfe and is. read. Doe ∫hut them∫elues and are.
P. 8 l 3. ᴛᴏ giue thy ∫elfe read. to giue thy fle∫h.
P. 16. l. 10. aw-like read. aulike.
P 64. l. 1. Peacefullie aduance. read. pace-fully aduance.

A Fig for Fortune:

Efted in fable vale, exild from Ioy,
I rang'd to feeke out a propitious place
Where I might fit and defcant of annoy
And of faire Fortune, altered to difgrace,
 At laft, euen in the confines of the night
 I did difcerne aloofe a fparkling light.

Then fet I fpurres vnto my Melancholie,
A Iade wheron I had ridden many a mile,
Which leffe then in the twinkling of an eye,
Brought me vnto that fatall lights beguile :
 Where I might fee an agonizing beaft,
 Bleeding his venym blood out at his breft.

His vpper fhape was faire-Angelicall,
The reft belowe, all whollie Serpentine,
Cole-blacke incroching vpon his pectorall,
And rudely inrowlled in a Gorgon-twine,
 His eyes like Goblins stared heer and there,
 In fell difdayne of fuch diffigured geare.

A FIG FOR FORTVNE.

At laſt he fpi'd me, and ſtaring on my face,
He rear'd his mongrel-lumpe vp towards me,
Fainting and falling in his Deaths-difgrace,
And yet enforcing ſtill more ſtabbes to die,
   Then thus he vauntingly began to tell me
   Of ſuch his fortitude in aduerſitie.

Welcome deer gueſt (quoth he) to *Catoes* Ghoſt,
Welcome true witneſſe of my fortitude,
Seeſt thou not how this hell-blacke ſhape almoſt
Hath quite ſubdu'd my vpper-albitude?
   It is aduerſitie vpon my ſtate,
   Which ſee how I reuenge it defperate.

With that, as with a new ſupplyed flood
The angrie ſtreame beares quite adowne the riuer
All obſtacle with vnappeaſed mood:
So his enraged hand did fierce deliuer
   Freſh death-ſtabbes to his loath'd mortalitie
   Euen at the naming of aduerſitie.

And then in four-fold mifconforted voyce
Of Life and Death : Rage and Difdaine, he added :
Whilom I was a man of *Romes* reioyce
Whiles happy Fortune my eſtate vppropped :
   But once when *Cæſar* ouer-topped all,
   Then (loe) this mid-night ſhape did me befall.

                      Then

Then gan I to conceipt my Cenſure-ſhip,
My Senatorie-pomp, and libertie
All baſe-ſubjeɛted to his Tyrant-whip:
My mind was mightie againſt ſuch miſerie,
   And rather would I die magnanimous
   Then liue to ſee a *Cæsar* ouer vs.

It was ynough that the Theſſalian fieldes
Suckt vp the mutuall bloud-ſhed of our men,
That *Pompey* dies, and all the Empire yeeldes
To *Cæſars* dauncing Fortune, and O*men*:
   Cato muſt die as free from ſeruitude
   As he diſdaineth *Cæſars* altitude.

Yet for my Countrey is a part of me,
And it is all ſubjeɛted to diſgrace,
Loe, that's my ſerpentine obſcuritie
For which I ſpight, and ſpit on Cæſars face,
   And ſtab me with a quaint diſdaine and anger
   Becauſe I will not liue in Cæſars danger.

Thou therefore that doeſt ſeem a dolefull wight,
View me the preſident of Cares redreſſe,
And if that Fortune be aboue thy might
Yet death is in thy power and readineſſe:
   Diſdaine Misfortune then t'inſult vpon thee
   Seeing that to die is all ſo faire and eaſie.

               B 2   Death

Death is miſſortunes monarchizing foe,
Prime Nature of Almightie fortitud,
Eternall Sanctuarie from vnreſt and woe,
Fames Arke, and all our frailties Period :
   Our lyfes true touchſtone, natures offertory,
   And bridge to ſweet Eliziums eternitie.

And as for baſe *Aduerſitie*, what is it ?
But Gloryes graue, a coward mindes ingalley,
The carrion of our lyfe, ſuppreſſe of ſpirrit,
Shadow of *Ioues* hate : Diſdaines obloquie,
   Helles ongate, an Owliſh conuerſation,
   All Ioyes depriſe, and ſorrowes invndation.

Looke not ſo downe agaſt at what I ſay,
But with a generous erected front,
Number theſe willing woundes (my hartes defray)
To Glory ſole land-ladie of this account :
   They are the Tythes I pay to eternall Fame :
   There is not any one of them prophane.

Be not injayld to baſe Aduerſitie,
Rather flip out thy life at gloryes windoe,
One ſtab will ſend thee to eternity,
And rid thee quite and cleane of all thy woe.
   Then there lies life-leſſe all Calamity,
   Thy name and Spirrit fayre amountes to glory.

It

There is no hell like to declined glorie,
Nor is *Prometheus* Vulture halfe fo fell
As the fad memorie of a happie ftorie
To him, that in aduerfitie doeth dwell :
  Ah, let him die that is not as he was,
  With ending bleffe breake he the houre-glaffe.

What booteh it to liue in bafe contempt
In euer melancholie-adumbred mood ?
A fable to the vulgar babblement,
A muddie ebbe after a Chryftall flood ?
  Out with thy candle, let it burne no more,
  When once thou art become the worlds eye-fore.

And tell not me of dutie vnto life ;
Nature is as indifferent to death,
Life led in joyes abandon and deprife
Is Natures deeper graue, then earth beneath :
  It is not death, that which the world calles dying,
  But that is death, which is all joyes denying.

Nature difdaines all groffe encountring meat
Fore-fed with N*ectar*, and Ambrofian fweetes,
And Night that is the merrie dayes defeat
We fee how Nature giues it drowfie greetes :
  Now : Sleep by night is but a filent figne
  How fweet it is to die in Ioyes decline.

                                        And

And then as is the morrowe-dawning day
A frefh re-bleffe to Natures next awake ;
So to the wretch that dies difgrace away
Elizium is his fecond lifes partake :
 Where he fhall triumph in eternity,
 And Fame the Chanteclere of fuch his glory.

Loe, I a prefident before thine eyes ;
This gore imports the glorie of my Ghoft,
Who but fore-weening Cæfars tyrannies
Fore-doom'd my felf in care-preuenting poft :
 Then thou that art a verie wretch indeed,
 Oh, why deferreft thou fo long to bleed ?

Out with that Iayle-bird of aduerfitie,
Difdaine to liue at Natures joyleffe leafure :
Bale drown'd in gore and magnanimitie
Is an vpdiue to all eternall pleafure :
 Thinke what a Fame-renowned thing it is
 In crimfon floods to warfare bafe de-bliffe.

Deferre no longer then thy doome of death,
But Champion-like confound Calamitie,
Profperities Satrap feares not to vnfheath
*H*is kil-care blade gainft flefhes fearful frailtie :
 Flefh of it felfe will one day turne to duft,
 Then doome it thou thy felfe fince fo it muft.

 Thou

Thou would'ſt not gladly eate an Abricocke,
Or Peache vnpar'd, becauſe their rinde is bitter,
And fear'ſt thōu then to giue thy ſelfe the ſtocke,
That ſo vnkindely bittereth all thy better?
   Oh, off with it, and yeeld thy ſweetes to *Ioue*,
   And he will counter-ſweete thee with his loue.

He will imboſome thee in his embrace,
And Ioye-embalme thee in his *H*eauen-delights,
Thy skarres and gaſhes he will faire-deface,
And ſanctifie thee with alhallowed rytes:
   Thou ſhalt be as a Meteor ouerſhining
   All mortall glory in her duſt declining.

There will we meet thee in Vermilion veſt,
I, *Otho, Anniball,* and all the reſt,
Fames choiſeſt Martyrs, who in Fates deteſt,
Doom'd all our ſelues to euerlaſting reſt.
   There will we magnifie thy happie woundes,
   And high applaud thē with Crownets & Crownes.

With that I drew out my emboldened blade,
Refolu'd to maſſacre my loathed life:
When (loe) the Ghoſt from out my ſight did vade,
As though to tell his *Ioue* of my ariſe:
   But ſuch a Sulphur ſtench hee left behind him
   That I in dreade thereof ſhooke euerie lim.

                           And

And therwithall my fword fell to the ground
And I mifdoubted fome illufion :
Such was the fafetie that then I found
In drowfie dread, and deaths confufion ;
   Prophanely fpoken : t'was no frailties deed,
   But God alonlie ftood thee then in fteed.

So then remounted on my Sable jade,
I rang'd ore craggy cliffes and defart dales
In way-leffe wander, and in Horrors fhade,
One while conceipting *Catoes* death-auailes,
   And then anon reflecting on his ftinke,
   Thus ftrayd I moft in dread & deaths inftinct.

Thrife drew I out my dagger for to ftab me
And then fo oft I muf'd why *Cato* ftunke fo,
Me thought there fhould no fuch difglory be
In facred Ghofts, freed from the filth of woe :
   So was my moody mindes perplexed wander
   Partial on lifes behalfe gainft deadly danger.

Then on I rode, and riding through a dale
Hell-like adumbred with a duskie gloome,
A fuddaine fatall blaft did me affaile
*A*nd droue me to a fecond damned doome,
   Where I might fee a more then hell-black finger
   That pointed me, and faid : Loe yonder, yonder.
           .C   With

With that my Melancholy ftar'd round about
And like a whirle-wind pofted to the place,
Where I might heare a voyce that roared out
Reuenge, reuenge, thy dollorous difgrace :
    And then eftfoons all in a Sulphur-flame
    Appear'd vnto my fight a fhape of fhame. .

*H*er face was skowle regarding on the ground,
Her eyes like *Heclas* euer-fparkling fires,
Her finger on her mouth was a dumbe bound
Of her *Cyclopian* frets and fell defires :
    In th'other hand fhe bare a fierie fheafe,
    *A*nd all her body was as pale as death.

*H*er haire was Snake-incurl'd *Medufa* like,
Hauing the power t'inftone me where I ftood :
So was I fenceleffe all but in diflike
And deadly horror of fo dread a Bug :
    At laft fhe fretted out an angry noife
    And thus infpeeched it into a voice.

Feare not my wan and moody mifproportion,
For (I confeffe) I am no fondlings joy,
Nor am I of a wanton difpofition
As is the God of Loue that idle boy,
    Yet am I a joy in another kind
    To fuch as in vn-ioy moft ioy doe find.

                                            I am

I am Reuenge, the doome of iniuries :
The Mifers refuge, and reuiue to bleffe
Occafions *Argus*, pith of Tragedies
The fumme of pollicie in all diftreffe :
　　Wrathes thunder-bolt, and triumph ouer thofe
　　That in their jollitie work others woes.

Th'injurious Gallant in his Commick braue
I agonize with vnexfpected bale,
Becaufe he fhall not thinke that in the graue
Lies nought but impotence and deaths auaile ;
　　I'le fhew him that the worme hath power to moue,
　　*A*nd none fo lowe but may amount aboue.

There is a Phœnix of *A*duerfitie
That faire refults from her incinderment,
And dares to braue with an vndaunted eie
Profperities fhine, & brighteft blandifhment :
　　It is Reuenge, t'is I can ftare it out,
　　And make it by difgrace the Mifers flout.

I rear'd *Corelian* from his exile ftate
To triumph ouer *Romes* ingratitude,
*A*nd *Cæfar* I did whollie animate
To down with *Pompeys* fcornfull altitude,
　　*H*is fute deni'd him by the Senate-houfe,
　　Did caufe me make him *Rome*-Emperious.

Of latter dayes a *Bourbon* in difgrace
I arm'd againft his Lieges injurie,
*A*nd gaue him victorie at *Pania* chace
Where he beheld him in captiuitie :
    What though he were a Traitor in fo doing,
    Tis ftatelie done. to ouer-top a King.

To be faire Fortunes euer Carpet-darling.
Is femall glorie : But Reueng'd difgrace
That's truly Mafculine, and rich triumphing :
*A*l peace-content is too too cheap and bafe :
    What manhood is it ftill to feed on Chickins.
    Like infant nurfe-boys in nice Fortunes kitchins ?

Giue me the man that with vndaunted.fperit
Dares giue occafion of a Tragedie :
*A*nd be content for his more after-merit
To be downe beaten from felicity :
    To th'end that with a fierce amount he may
    Re-bleffe himfelfe in fpight of Fortunes nay,

T'is braue to plunge adowne into the deep
*A*nd fo vp-bound againe aboue the waue,
To be continually a mountain-fheep
Is Cockrell-like, it is a dung-hill braue :
    The crauin Cocke is hartleffe from his hill,
    Shame to be fo that haft a manly will.

                            To

To be depof'd from bliffe by injurie,
Is double glorie to remount to it,
Nor is thy title loft to dignitie
Vnleffe fuppreffe of fpirite forfeit it:
   Misfortunes power cannot foyle thy right,
   Doe thou but beare a minde in her defpight.

We cannot fay that man is ouercome
That ftill beares vp his arme againft his foe,
Nor that he is fincerely out-run
Whom the Corriuals trip doth ouerthrow:
   VVhat ere is loft with fore-wits vnpreuention,
   Win it againe with after-wits contention.

This humane fate, fometime to flip and fall,
But to ingrouell in durt is beaftlie bafe:
To rife againe, oh that is Iouiall,
Or els reuenge to death the downe-difgrace:
   Therefore, thou haft a fpirit of defpight,
   As well as in good hap to take delight.

The gallant man vnhorft amidft his foes
Fightes to the death his lateft wrath away,
And when he can no more: with mops and mowes
*H*e floutes both them, and Death, and Deftinie:
   So if not Victor, yet vnvanquifhed
   *H*e dies to euerlafting liuelihed.

C 3

Be

Be not as is the coward *Scorpion*
That rounded all about with aſhie embers
Diſpaires and dies in ſelfe deſtruction
Renting with fierce enrage his venym members :
   But if that *Ioue* nill ayde thy fortitude
   Downe to all *Acharon,* and the Furie brood.

Hell holdes in honor the braue minded man
That knowes the price and value of his head,
That meaſures not Renowne by inch or ſpan,
But by th'eternitie of *Ioues* Godhead,
   That ſkornes to brooke baſe infelicitie,
   Or pocket vp degraded dignitie.

And haply *Ioue* himſelfe ſupplants thy ſtate
To ſee how thou canſt ſcamble vp againe,
And ſcuffle manly with malignant fate
To a redoubled glories rich attaine :
   Then cheerly man : inhearten all thy ſperrites
   And dead Reuenge thy miſeries demerites.

Loe, I thy Aduocate vnto the Hagges
Will ſtill importune thy Proſperitie,
And be at hand with poiſon, and with dagges
To execute each plotted tragedie :
   Misfortune ſhall not ſcoffe at thy confuſion,
   If hell and I befriend thee in coniunction.

                          Lay

Lay but thy hand vpon thy confcience.
And faire in-vow mee in an earneft fpirit,
So fhalt thou compaffe Tragick confequence
On all thy foes that now fo frollick it.
 They fhall no longer feaft vpon thy frets
 Nor regifter thy woes in their banquets.

Thou fhalt eniowle them one againft another
With hoftill jealoufie, and dead debate :
I tell thee (man) all friendfhip is unfure
Founded vpon anothers downe eftate :
 Nor ioyes he long againft Reuenges doome,
 That wrong in-ftates him in anothers roome.

*H*eauen is the Arbiter, and wils it fo,
I and the Furies are the inftruments
To act that iuftice in all tragicke woe,
Now is it in this cafe our good intents
 To ioyne with vs thy manuall act heerin
 That more then priftin glory thou maift win.

But fay thou winne not priftin glory by it
Yet fhalt thou fee thy foes in downe difgrace,
Thy felfe fhalt act it, fuch fhall be thy merit,
And fuch thy glorie in a higher place :
 What greater glorie can betide the Vale
 Then force the Mountaine-top adowne to fall ?
         So

So fhall thy glorie not be loft, but left,
Yea loffe to them that all fo dearly buy it,
When thou fhalt Phœnix-like of bliffe bereft
Rife from thy ruines to a higher merit :
 Degraded from a puppit Commicke-ftage
 To act the ftatelie Tragick perfonage.

Chang'd to a faire enfiered *S*alamander
Breathing Reuenges bright and facred flames,
Which high infpirits men to lofty matter
In quaint difdaine of aulicke infant games ;
 Games of the bodie, follies of the minde,
 Oh, how t'is bafe to liue fo like a Hinde.

Nature hath giuen you male and female willes,
The one wherwith to couet meriments,
The other to deteft all aduerfe ils,
Now is almightie *Ioues* great woonderments
 More in his Thunder-boltes then in his fweetes,
 To fhew Reuenge more woorth then Pleafures greets.

Then arme thy felfe Reuenges Champion,
To bandie away thy foes, and all difgrace
VVith polliticke difsimulation
Of contrarie language, and contrary face :
 As the Camelion changeth ftill his hue
 VVith euery obiect cullor : fo change thou.

        So

So maiſt thou cloſe Camelion-like conceale
Thy tragicke ſhape of Horror and Reuenge,
Whiles' they miſdoubting not thy falſe reueale
*A*re caught vnwares like Woodcocks in a ſprenge,
    Such is the honour of Aduerſitie,
    With ſleightes to vndermine Proſperitie.

Be to thy oath, as th'Ape is to his blocke,
Sometimes ſticke to it, ſometimes flit from it
As pregnant pollicy may thee prouoke :
T'is foole-ſincerity, and want of wit
    To make a pot to breake thy head withall,
    Or rather not to break it firſt of all.

Vſe Friend and Foe, and Neuter all alike,
Onlie as inſtrumentall implements
To thy deſigne ; thy aymed ſtroke to ſtrike :
And ſee them but with ayery complements :
    That done, and thy affaire effeɛted,
    Deſtroy them all for feare thou be deteɛted.

Dead dogges barke not, nor ſtands it with thy honour
To be vpbrayded with a curteſie ;
Much leſſe to be employd in like deuoir
According *Quid pro Quoes* ſeruilitie :
    Such is the ſumme of perfeɛt pollicie
    To worke ſecurely with Vulgaritie.
           D   Be

Be clofe, and iealous in each action
For that clofe dealing is good Speeds affurãce ;
And Iealoufie's the Sentinell of Caution ;
And bear thou ftill in mind this circumftance ;
   If all good fortune, and aduife fhall faile thee
   To haue a ftarting hole for after-fafetie.

T'was meger Prudence in the antique Sages
That but with Goodnes could recure an Euill :
Giue me the man that with wittes pollices
Can Saint a Deuill with another Deuil :
   That can fo fhift, and fhuffle the cards in fift,
   As turne vp whatfoeuer Trump he lift.

T'is Heauens attaine to fend thy foes to Hell
With mutuall murthers in *S*editions field :
The vpper Buckets fall into the well
The lowers faire amount we fee doth yeeld :
   Such is the merit of Reuenges deed,
   With others wrack to work thine own good fpeed.

At leaft to die in well appeafed wrath
And in furuiue of all thine enemies
Is ftately dying : t'is faire lie downe and laugh,
And an vp-rife to *Ioues* benignities,
   E*lizium* and Fame in after ages,
   Reuenges bleffed Rightes and *A*ppennages.

                        Then

Then come, imbrace me with a firme aſſent
And thinke no idle voyce ſollicits thee ;
I tell thee (man) in thy arbitrement
Lies all thy glorie, and felicitie :
  I'le be thy hand-maid heer in earth belowe,
  The reſt aboue great *Ioue* he will beſtow.

So ſayd, ſhe rear'd her skowle down-looke on
*A*nd vagranlie regarding round about
In Period-pawſe ; At laſt as one beſtraught
She ſtar'd, and trembled, and began to powt
  And ſuddenly ſhe vaniſht out of fight
  Becauſe now in the Eaſt it dawn'd day-light.

Euen ſo (quoth I) is it Reuenges guize
To be in force by Night, be gone by Day ?
Such is not the inſtinkt of Paradize,
God graunt it be no Plutonicke affray :
  Oh what it is to be a mortall man
  Subiekt to all the guiles and ſleights of Satan.

Yet for her ſpeech was conſonant to Nature,
I wiſht ſh'had been an Oracle of truth ;
So credulous is *A*ngers moodie vigure
When once it is in-Cæſared in youth :
  And hand in-handed with a quaint Diſdaine
  Iniurious diſglorie to ſuſtaine.
D 2

Yea

Yea what is not the mifer apt to doe,
What not beleeue to mittigate his euill ?
Well may he faine a patient outward hue,
But not exile his inward damned deuill,
   The Vulture of defpite that neuer dies
   But rents and teares his heart in rauin-wife.

Now Chanteclere the vigill of the night
Crew broad day-light : when *Titan* in the Eaft
Peece-meale appearing in his priftin bright
Broad-waked euery creature, man and beaft,
   Ech mufick-bird bebleffing his amount
   Both in the humble vale and haughtie mount.

When (loe) my jade vnfprighted, and vnnighted,
Rag'd and engag'd himfelfe to all aduenture
Ore hedge, and ditch, and flood, fo fell affrighted
He was to fee the Sunne, fo fhone a creature :
   All as the Tench in waterles defpaire
   Beateth himfelfe to death in fpight of ayre.

So on I hafted at my jades beheft,
As whilom *Phaeton* in his skyey carte,
Weake (God he knowes) to rule fo fierce a beaft,
Deadly feare-frighted both in harte and arte :
   But whome our Lords fafe prouidence befpeedeth,
   No humane power of heart or arte he needeth.

                            At

At laſt in proceſſe of an ouer-tire
My moody beaſt ſtood ſtill in palſie-wiſe,
Trembling and fainting in a daunted ire,
(Such is the end of Rages ryotize :)
    Then had I leaſure for to looke about me,
    And (loe) I ſpide a Rock in ſhining glorie.

I hy'd me to it with a pleaſing pace,
And yet not pleaſant, for t'was all too ſlow :
So flight is Melancholie to darke diſgrace
And deadly drowſie to a bright good morrow ;
    Yet on I march'd, and marueil'd at the fight,
    I neuer in all my life ſaw thing ſo bright :

As more and more I neer'd vnto the place
So by degrees my Melancholy fainted,
When (loe) anon with a religious pace
A ſnow-white Iennet towards me aduanced :
    His name was *Good deſire,* his ſaddle greene
    Was *Reuerend Solace* of a godly ſpleen.

Whereat my jade affrighted and deſpighted
Sped all to naught as myſt before the Sonne :
When I eftſoons internallie delighted
Was rapt by *Good deſire* vnto *Deuotion* :
    A penall place, yet parcell of the rock,
    And brighter then the Noony Zodiack.

D 3

There

There kneel'd a reuerend *S*ophie all in teares
With needle-pointed Difcipline correcting
His Flefhes frailtie : Oh how he befmears
The place with penall bloud, and blubbering :
   *H*is hart was wholly fixt on Chrift his Paffion,
   So fhew'd his Crucifixe-contemplation.

Before him was a Death's-head full of wormes,
The picture of a Graue, and an Hower-glaffe,
A map of Doomfday, and *H*ell in fearfull formes,
And Heauen figur'd all in *S*aintlie follace :
   *H*is pale and megre countenance areeded
   His fpare poor fare, and how hard he bedded.

Standing behind him, he was in a trance,
*A*nd I betooke my Eie to a fteddie gaze,
My Mind to an amaze at fo great fuffrance,
So penall fuffrance in fo bright a place,
   *A*nd now I fee (faid I) there is a bliffe
   Euen in Aduerfitie what ere it is.

And thus afide I argued the cafe :
In place fo bright what meane thefe drearements ?
A heauie cafe deferues a dolefull place
Since bale and bleffe are aduerfe Complements :
   *A*nd yet the Glowe-worme in the darkeft night
   Though blacke it be, fhines foorth a ftarry bright.

                                 Cato

Cato and Reuenge were blacke, and both to blame
Th'one in fulphure ftenche, th'other in Lights abhorr,
And Melancholye was the Iade of fhame
That darkeling brought me to that dnbble dorr;
  A better horfe I hope hath brought me hether
  For both the place is bright, and tis fayr weather.

Long haue I rang'd to finde a place of eafe
Whear I may paffe away my penfiue playntes,
And happly if this be now that place of peace
Heer reft I euer in my woes attayntes:
  Heer in this Caue, and in this fable fhrowde
  Dye I a Caytiffe, vnder Fortunes clowd.

This aged man and I will both together
Complaine in common our calamytie;
That haply whiles we ftriue t'outplaine each other
Suche our ambition may fwage our miferie,
  Or both at once, may cracke as ouerftrained,
  Ambitious dying is a glorie gained.

But (well I wot) thou wrong'ft this holy place
By mif-conftruȼting it to care and bale,
T'is puddle facrilege fo to difgrace
The grace of God, through errors rude mifprifall:
  What though the man doe feeme difconfolate,
  Somewhat it is doth thee exhilerate.

                             For

For why, I felt my fpirit all poffeft,
With a reuiued hope to happineffe ;
It was the Grace of God in my vnreft
That in-lie cheer'd me vp to future bleffe,
   Deer gift of God, the Charaſter of life
   And heauenly make-peace of our ghoftly ftrife.

It is the Raye, and Speech of heauen to **man,**
The Rainebowe-pledge of Gods beneuolence,
The Limbecke of our juftice, and the Fan
That winnoweth fin away from innocence :
   Prime moouer, and efficient caufe of good
   To all that are redeem'd with Chrift his blood.

Whiles thus with infant-zeale I did applaud
The in-come grace of God into my heart
In full deteft of fore-affeſted fraud,
Loe, now this penall Sage began to ftart
   From out his trance, and with a heauenlie voyce
   And armes a croffe, he bid his foule rejoyce.

Reioyce (quoth he) at this eternall truth,
The man is bleft that for Gods juftice fake
Suftaincs with Patience reproch and ruth,
Our Lord hath promift that he wil partake
   His heauen to him : *H*is name be praif'd therfore,
   And fo he kift the Croffe, and faid no more.

With

With that my heart exulted in my breaft,
As faire prefaging weale vnto my woe ;
For why I was not vulgarlie diftreft
But, for a caufe that bore an honeft fhowe,
　Yet for my frailtie was impatient
　I long'd for fpeedy death or folagement.

Then ftept I to that man of Myfteries
With carefull Complement leaft to offend,
When he eftfoons with reuerend arife
Did recomplie me like a perfect friend :
　The teares of joy that trill'd adowne his chin
　Did fweare what true affection was within.

And laftly he thus embracingly befpake me,
Welcome (*Elizian*-man) a thoufand fold
More deere and fhone to *Catechryfius* eye
Then all the Pleafant pride of Pearle or Gold :
　Rare, yea all too rare are now adayes
　Elizas fubjects feen to paffe this wayes.

Belike yee are a Paradized people
That fo contain your felves in home-delights,
As though that only vnder your fteeple
And no wher els were all May-merry Rights :
　A bleffed people ye are, if it be fo
　And yet me thinkes thou feem'ft a man of woe.
　　　　　　E　　　　　　　　Whereto

Wherto I anfwered all with humble thanks:
Firft, that I was the man he took me for
Bred and brought vp on fayre *Elizas* bankes,
Next, did I largely fhew him furthermore
How bleffedly we liue, as hee had heard
Vnder *Elizas* peacefull power and guard.

*A*nd as for my peculiar diftreffe,
I tolde him fo I feem'd, and fo I was
The Rag of Fortune : Badge of bafe debleffe,
The *S*punge of care, a broken Hower-glaffe :
The Finger-man of fhame, and Obloquie
Downly degraded from Felicitie.

I told him of my dreary journement
On moodie Melancholie ; and how I fped
With *Cato*, and Reuenges babblement,
And how, along the Defart as I fled
I met with *Good* D*efire* a goodly Steed
That brought me thether in my ghoftly need.

I would haue told him more of my arange
Euen all the verie confcience of my cafe,
*T*he caufe of fuch my reprobate exchange
From bleffe to bale : & how frŏ place to place
Bowndleffe in care, I rang'd to bownd my Fate,
Content to die : but not die defperate.

But

But he eftſoones preuented me, and ſaid :
Oh happie thou, if ſo thou knew'ſt thy hap,
I tell thee (man) thou art right faire apaid
Exild from *Mammon* into *Ieſus* lap :
   Come fit we downe, and I will ſhew thee how
   In this diſtreſſe, thou mayſt nor breake, nor bow.

So downe we ſate : my heart was feſtiuall
My eare was eager-liquoriſh to embaite
Good *Catechryſius* his Cordiall :
Who then with eies to heauen eleuate
   And croſſe-laid armes did vow ſyncerely
   *A*ll loue and truth in what he meant to ſhew me.

And then (quoth he) deare Engliſhman, ſuppoſe
Me not vnciuill t'interrupt thy tale,
For in our Lord I well aread thy woes
And Charitie hies me to recure them all :
   Now all is but the action of the Mind,
   That rectifi'd, the reſt is all but wind.

Know then, thou art no better then a man
Natur'd indifferently, to weale or woe,
Who ere he be that's borne of a woman
Is firſt juſt nothing, next an **Embrio**,
   Then borne into the world in impotence
   Poore intereſt to future Excellence.

E 2

Nay

Nay borne in fable finne to Gods offence,
Nipt in the bloffome by the blaft of Hell,
Spur-gall'd of *Adam* both in foule and fence
And hodge-podged betwcen a man & Deuel,
   A fardle of frailties doom'd vnto damnation
   So fore we haue incurr'd Gods indignation.

If thefe be titles of felicitie,
Ah, poore fclicitie, vnpleafant Pride :
Rooted in hell, brancht in mortalitie
And round imbark'd with fin on euerie fide :
   Nor are we thus difgrac'd but of our felfes
   For firft we eate the Apple of all thefe helles.

We might have chofen in *Adams* Libertie
Whether t'haue eate that Apple yea or no,
But needs we would aduenture : And wot you why ?
Forfooth of Pride both good and bad to know :
   So flunke from vs the glorie and grace of God
   Leauing vs quite to our felfe breeching-rod

Heerhence we couet counterfeit content,
Sublime mundanity, and our Flefhes eafe,
Rating the trafh of earth true folagement
*A*nd euery toy of price our fence to pleafe :
   Such is our frailtie, and yet we fee it not
   So to fubject vs to fo feruile Lot.

                         And

And fuch the matter of thy difcontent,
Becaufe thou ouer prizeſt Fleſhes fence,
Rating the world at all too high a rent
Wheras it is but duſt and Gods offence:
　　The *Mammon* of iniquitie in Scripture phrafe
　　And but a meere Crocadyle amaze.

Conceipt thy felfe no better then thou art,
A forie Iourney man from birth to death
And all this world but matter of vndefart
And a meere momentary traſh-bequeath:
　　Death doomes all Fleſh at laſt, and Fleſh-affaires
　　Be it Fleſhes joyes, or Fleſhes feruile cares.

Bleſſe being the perfe６t Counterpane of good
This world is not of worth to correfpond it
It being but traſh ore-flowne with Frailties flood
And deep indown'd from heauens fellowſhip:
　　Then vp to heauen amount thy true ambition
　　And as for earth out-care it in contrition.

Not to defpaire and die as *Cato* told thee,
For that is bafe Pufillanimitie
And Natures moſt unhallowed infamie,
Treafon to God, and fell difloyaltie
　　So to betray his Fort and Chara６ter
　　To felfe-mifdoome, and drearie difaſter.

E 3　　　　　　　　　　　　　We

We ought not cancell Gods eternall doome
Vn-labelling our life from his faire Charter,
For ſuch is diffidence in his holidoome
And prowde in-officing vs in his affaire :
   Nor can we kill Calamitie by death
   For he is juſt in earth, and hell beneath.

Thou canſt not flit from his almightie doome
*H*e being th'Arbiter of all, and nothing :
Who gaue thee Eſſence out of V*acuum*
Can paine thy aſhes all in earth repoſing :
   Well maiſt thou ſhift his anger into grace
   But not depriue thee from his heauenly face.

As vaine it is to thinke Reuenges deed
Can counter-doome thy bale to bleſſedneſſe,
The power of Fleſh being but a rotten reed
And ſelfely inclined vnto all diſtreſſe :
   Then ſince we are ſo wretched of our ſelfes
   Add worſe to yll doth but encreaſe our helles.

Such is Reuenge : It is a haggard yll,
A Luciferiall ranke uncharitie :
The venym, and blacke-*Santus* of our will
Vnreaſons rage ; ſpawne of Impietie,
   Breath of Deſpaire, Prime-brat of Enuies brood,
   And all good Natures *Satyr-Antipode.*

                             Reuenges

Reuenges arme rear'd vp againſt the Foe
Aimes to defeat God of his intereſt
Who clauſually reſeru'd that worke of woe
Vnto his owne judiciall beheſt ;
   Thou art a man, and once didſt ſucke thy mother,
   Thou canſt not judge thy ſelfe, much leſſe another.

And what know'ſt thou whether haply for thine owne
Or for thy Predeceſſors ſinnes thou ſuffereſt,
God oft transfers his indignation
From the offending Eaſt to th'ending Weſt.
   Or whether it be to trie thy patience,
   And fluſh the more thy good obedience.

If it be for thy ſinnes, oh happy thou
That art ſo temporally corre</dted :
Such is Gods mercy, not his Iuſtice-blow,
A worſer doome is to thy euill indebted :
   For God being good in all infinitie
   Such is thy ſinnes, and hels affinitie.

And if for thy forefathers treſpaſſes,
T'is braue to be ſo good a Sacrifice,
God earſt to expiate thy amiſſes
Being a preſident before thine eies
   Of willing death ; wee are not borne only
   Vnto our ſelfes : Suche is vncharitie.
                             The

The feeble Nature euen of Flefh and Blood
Hath been fo kind to die for Anceftrie,
Gentility records *Eneas* good
In that he bore his aged fathers frailtie
    Through *Troyes* flames : much more ought Charitie
    Beare patiently anothers penaltie.

But fhall I fay that haplie in this cafe
Our Lord is pleaf'd to trie thy patience,
Thy valure, and obedience in difgrace ?
Oh, that were all too glorious a pretence :
    For (well ye wot) that Souldiour is a King
    That choycelie is employ'd in warfaring.

T'is *Scowndrell*-glorie ftill to fit at eafe
In gawdie fatisfaction of thy fence :
Nay, t'is no glorie at all, but a difeafe
That Canker-like confumes thine Innocence.
    Now God being pleaf'd to cure thee thereof
    Doth thus confound it all into a fcoffe.

And yet confounds it fo, as thou maift fee
His Iuftice and his Mercie ioind together,
Thy yll contrould to future dignitie,
So dooth the goodneffe of thy caufe auerre :
    If God did meane thy eternall infamie,
    Worfe paffiue caufe had foule befall'n thee.

                           Thou

Thou canſt not haue a more aſſured pawne
Of Gods benignitie then a good cauſe,
It being vnto thy ſoule a ſacred dawne
Of heauens day; and an eſpeciall clauſe
  Or Charter-warrant of Saluation
  By a ſecure Conſcience-atteſtation.

Not all the glorie of this world is worth
The minnim-*Emphefis* of a good conſcience:
The verie penall teares it ſendeth foorth
Are more then pearles of Indie-excellence :
  Much more are they Emperiall dignities
  Her inward Ioyes and Iocundities.

Say that the Corpes of ſuch a Conſcience
Lie all in mange before the Miſers dore,
His name as hell held in the worlds offence,
Yet is he not vnfortunate therefore ;
  For heauen and he being ſtill in good conjunĉtion
  All that's but vapor, and no ſound confuſion.

Nay t'is to thee a haughtie merit-matter
If brookt with patient valure to the end ;
Which eaſely thou maiſt doe, if thou conſider
That Ieſus tempts thy patience as a friend,
  Not in his rage aboue thy power and ſtrength,
  Whom he reprooues at firſt, he ſaues at length.

                                 *A*nd

And footh to fay, what is Profperitie
That fo fhould make thee abhor Aduerfitie?
Euen *Cæfars* loftie pomp, and foueraigntie
Is not by ods fincere felicitie ;
   Subiect to Care and Alteration
   Through Enuie, Errour, and *A*dulation.

How much adoe is done ere men attaine
To wealth and glorie by *A*mbition?
Still carke and care fhares halfe the feruile gaine,
The reft remaines to Deaths confufion :
   T'is well if tart Synderifie and Hell
   Triumver not to towlle the pafsing-bell.

Care in attaining, and care in attaine
Care is the lower and the vpper ftaire :
Such carefull glorie is but glorious paine,
Yea care, or care-leffe either, all's but aire :
   Feaft it in care, or feaft it carelefly
   Death is the latter *Harpie* of all glory.

Befides, how many Villaines are aduanc'd
To fuch theatricall, and ftagic-ftate
Whilft Vertue lies obliuioufly entranc'd,
Neglected, and difdain'd as out of date :
   Befides the multiplicitie of abufe
   That is in fuch mundanities mif-ufe.

                              Whereas

Whereas the patient Satrap in diftreffe
Behonefteth his guiltie fuffrance :
And if he fuffer for Gods righteoufneffe,
Loe, there the fumme of all true valliance :
   Heauens *Machabe* he is that fo downe-dies
   Guiltie of all glorie, and Gods deere dainties.

Who heares his name a thoufand yeeres hence
Will giue it glorie, praife, and reuerence
*A*s to a Temples ruin-Monuments
Rafed in *S*acrilege, and Gods offence *:*
   He will be-villaine thofe that did the deed
   *A*s *S*cowndrell-*A*gents of *H*ells blacke areed.

We are not borne to Fortunes complements,
As foueraigne dainties ; but as Vertues tooles
Wherwith to fhape vs perfect lineaments
Of honorable Manhood *:* And not as Fooles
   To dote vpon the Penfill in our hand
   *A*nd not depaint vs like to Gods command.

Vertue's the Ladie of our humanitie,
And Fortune but the hand-maid of our merit,
Now, were it homelie done to magnifie
The meane aboue the maine : T'were pettie fperit
   To flip our nettes into the Sea for water
   And pardon Fifh, as no part of the matter.

      This

This life is but a warfare againſt ſinne
And either Fortune is but ſinnes Coate-armour,
Be it bright or blacke, great danger lies therein
If thou reſiſt not with a haughtie valour :
    T'is witleſſe yeelding to her gawdements,
    And cowardize vnto her drearements.

What skils it whether we fight with blacke or white
If blacke and white be both our enemies,
The one in guile, th'other in flat deſpight ?
The Goblin-Bugs, and Faery Hiedegies
    Are both the ſhades of hell, and night-aſſrayes
    Encounter, nor aſſent quelles their dlſmayes.

And why are we the image of our God
The Monarches ouer all Elementaries ?
But to controwll with Reaſons righteous rod
All fleſh and bloods fraile ſenſualities ;
    T'is ſenſualitie, and pettie power
    To mal-content thee for a fading flower.

Stand thou on Reaſons haughty Promontorie
Superiour and ſecure ouer all diſgrace,
Rage wind, and waue, & horror round about thee
Yet all is glorie and peace in that bright place :
    Nor Death, nor Hell can damnifie thy honer
    So long as Reaſons arme beares vp thy banner.

                           Oh

Oh generous minded men that can efteeme
All ftate inferiour to their mindes degree,
And not abandon it to bafe mifdeeme
Of any Fortunes power aboue her glee :
 But can out-ftare it with a quaint regard
 In reference to merite, and Gods grand reward.

That can conceipt all Fortune as a Fog
Bee't black or bright, all but a matter of aire,
If bright, oh then it doth but flatter and cog,
If blacke, it drowns thee with a flood of care,
 Vnleffe thy mind be as a Sunne aboue it
 Faire ouer-fhining all her mift-demerit.

Faire Fortune is a Bog, a dauncing danger,
And Temperance muft foot it with a modeft pace ;
Her frowne, a gulfe that drownes the hartleffe ftranger
That cannot wend with Patience his difgrace ;
 Both that and it are mortuarie matter
 If fed vpon in Indifcretions platter.

Submit not then thy facred Subftantiue
To Fortunes heftes : but as thou art of Nature,
So ftill continue thy prerogatiue
Aboue her blandifhing and fpightfull power,
 So fhone a Patrimonie as thy Mind
 Let neuer Fortune waft it out of kind.

F 3

Thou

Thou art no part of Fortune, but thine owne :
Vertue thy fore-guide, Heauen thy attaine,
Good death, not loftie life thy beſt Renowne,
Contented mind thy glories after-gaine :
  Without content all glorie is but gall,
  *A*nd with content diſgrace is feſtiuall.

Content's the Spunge of true felicitie,
The Cordiall againſt degraded bleſſe,
Corriuall to the higheſt Empirie,
The badge of Innocence and Righteouſneſſe,
  Vertues enthrone, Rent of a manlie mind
  To God for whatſoeuer ſtate afsign'd.

It is the *Phœnix* of fore-glories Embers :
Patience her wing, *H*eauen is her amount,
It is the *Chriſtopher* whoſe manly members
Waſteth the miſer-man through all affrount,
  It is the true and perfeᴄt *Salamander,*
  Breathing vitalitie in flames of fire.

Not ſo the Skowndrell in his greateſt glorie,
For ther is no Content in guilt of euill,
A skowll down-looke, and ſwart ſynderiſie
Betokening him a member of the Deuill :
  He cannot with a faire erected front
  Be-*Abba* God : nor yeeld him good accompt.

                                        His

44

His glorie in guilt of yll is as a flower
Begnawne with an accurſed Caterpiller,
Or as an Apple periſht in the coure
Though faining outwardlie a faithfull faire ;
   Oh fatall incenſe, oh accurſed fume
   That ſo choaks vp the wretch doth it aſſume.

Wheras the others conſcientiall-content
Doth feaſt his Fates, and ciuillize their rage,
Turning their gall to glee and ſolagement
And faire be-heauening hell with her aſſwage ;
   *H*ee's as a Bwoy aboue the boſterous waue
   Dauncing to ſcorne the Seas ybillowy-braue.

So ſtrong in power is his ſincere incline
To Gods ordaine and holie prouidence,
Reſting therin as in a ſacred ſhrine
Or Sanctuarie againſt all hels offence :
   The Deuils eager-gripe cannot confound
   Him whom our Lords protection doth bound.

There is no hell but in our Gods offence :
Pleaſe him, and boldlie plunge adowne the deep
Of all accurſe : his holy Prouidence
Being the *Argus* which doth neuer ſleep,
   Will on the wings of ſafe Protection
   Still beare the juſt man vp from all perdition.

                            What

What hap can hap amiſſe to Gods bebleſt?
What waue can ſurge aboue his prouidence?
The *H*agges of hell are chain'd to his beheſt
*H*ell gates obey his high omnipotence:
   Diue downe to Hell, if he beare vp thy chin
   Wel maiſt thou ſink a while, nere drowne therein.

If once thy hope be anchored in God
No waue, no bluſter can endanger thee,
Thy foot from falling is ſecurely ſhod
He correſponding thy fidelitie:
   If God thy Center be and thy defence
   Be Hell, be Deuil thy Circumference.

The Tyrants ſteele, the Hang-mans Axeltree,
*H*is ſtrangles, mangles, and his fierie doomes
Cannot confound true magnanimitie
Founded on Gods true loue & hollidoomes;
   His life in gore, his Ghoſt in ſhades of hell
   *A*re more at eaſe than anie tongue can tell.

The earthen minded man cannot conceaue
So haughtie glorie in diſglorie and dole:
His groueling appetite doth ſo bereaue
*H*is wit, impelling it to another gole;
   Hee's ſo beſotted in his Leproſie
   That it alonlie he eſteems true glorie.

                                   But

But time will come when at a iuſt Tribunall
The iuſt mans miſerie, and the miſers glee
Will come in *Coram*, and bee doom'd for all :
Then mourning good ſhall mount to Maieſtie,
   *A*nd ſin-polluted glorie downe diſcend
   T'irreparable dollour without end.

Then væ to guiltie glorie, glorious guilt,
Væ to ſuppreſſe of vertue, aduance of vice ;
The Raſcalls towre on Vertues ruines built
Muſt then adowne, and he repent the price :
   Oh, farre more happie then diſgraced good,
   Then Vice aduanc'd to skowndrell altitud.

But thou wilt ſay it is Detraction,
It is thy name defam'd among the juſt
Thy life bely'd through miſconſtruction
That more then all thy glorie in the duſt
   Be-hels and tortureth thy manly mind,
   It being a miſchiefe of a woorſer kind.

Bee't ſo (*Elizian*-man) I doe confeſſe
Detraction is indeed a monſtrous euell,
Foule *Harpie* of honour, Night of righteouſneſſe
And the vnciuill tongues moſt venym-driuell,
   Much more I doe confeſſe it is a ſpight
   To be of honeſt men a villaine hight.

              G   But

But on the other fide, when thou confider
The fand-blind errors euen of jufteft men,
*H*ow much from Gods intuitie they differ
And oft when moft they iudge, are moft miftaken ;
   Difpaire not at their doomes, but in thy hart
   Bleffe God who fees thee inly what thou art.

Oft-times the good man credits with his eares
Not with his eyes : Therhence if injurie
Redownd to thee ; the fault being whollie theirs,
Farre be it from thy hearts fynderifie :
   Yea rather with a bolt-vp countenance
   Giue it the Lie, and hardie fufferance.

Much more the Villaines obloquie difdaine it
As currifh crauin againft thy Innocence,
His Viper-language cannot cracke thy credit
A blufh-leffe confcience pleading thy defence ;
   *H*is tongue againft thy Soules fecure eftate
   Fares as a reed againft a brazen gate.

But if his obloquie be a true *Eccho*
Of thy mif-gouernance and guilty life,
Then well I doe aread it is a woe
Vnto thy honor, and a flaughter knife ;
   Wheras contrarie-wife if thou be found
   It's but an ayrie, and an idle fownd.

                                Faire

Faire then aguize thee with a trim tranfcent
Aboue al flefh and hells indignitie,
Emboft with gentle Patience, and Content
Lamb-like repineleffe at aduerfitie,
　　For, footh I fay, and heauen will witneffe it
　　The juft mans miferie is a haughtie merit.

*A*nd firft pleafe God in his commandements,
Next, with a true Satrapick-fufferance
Grace me that face of thine, thofe lineaments
*A*gainft Detraction and hells mif-valiance,
　　Shew that thou art the image of thy God
　　In patient portage of his penall rod.

*S*o, nor difpaire, nor yet reuenge thy woe
But with the prudent Serpent in diftreffe
*S*afe-garde thy head; let die the reft beloe:
Thy head in heauen, thy heele in heauineffe
　　Is merrie matter, if thou well confider
　　That death rejoynes them both in bleffe togither.

Haft thou not noted this effect in Nature,
How chill-cold winter calefies the water
Anteperiftezing her powers together
Wherby it faire refifts her ycie ire?
　　So, in thy winter of Aduerfitie
　　Create thy felfe a fommer-Iubilie.
　　　　　　　　G 2　　　　　　　　　Giue

Giue place to furie as the humble Snaile
Retreating in his hornes gainſt miſaduenture,
In time all violence will ſelfelie quaile
If vnprouok'd with curriſh miſdemeanure :
   *T*he chilleſt winter and the darkeſt night
   Redound at laſt to *S*ommer, and broad day-light.

See how the Marigold againſt the Son
Diſplayes and ſhuts it ſelfe at his dominion
Leſſening at night her ſpred proportion
But nere diſculloring her gold-complexion,
   *S*o to the ſoueraigntie of God aboue
   With Fortunes night deminiſh not thy loue.

But thinke misfortune is the flayle of grace,
The clarifying Fornace of thy ſoule
Wherewith God ſtrips away thy chaffe-diſgrace
And make thee pure mettle with ſuch controwlle
   T'is honorable manhood to obey thy God,
   Bee't in his mercie, or his juſtice-rod.

Wilt thou ſubmit thy mind to Fortunes Impoſtes
Faithleſſe of Gods benignitie and care ?
Ah, rather doe diſdaine her bales and boſtes
As Crocadyle-deceipts, and crabbed ware :
   And to thy God alonly plie thy heſt
   For ſuch is pure dutie, and the pure beſt.

                                So

So doing better boones then Fortunes baubles
Will Spaniell-like attend vpon thy merite,
Good death, and after death th'immoouables
Of glorie, and fame, and an in-heauened fpirite
   In euerlafting Iubilie and bleffe
   Far more then heart can thinke, or tongue expreffe. .

So fhalt thou fwim away in Vertues flood,
A happy burthen to a happy Maine,
Gods flowerie-eternitie garlanding thy good
And his embrace lullabying all thy paine :
   Oh, happy thou when fuch adoption
   Shall faire befall thy tribulation.

When all thy Croffes fhall appeare in heauen
As euer-memorable Annalles of thy merit,
Or as bright Trophees to thy Vertue geuen
The Saintes of glorie all applauding it ;
   When God with his fereneft countenance
   Shall euer bright be-boone thy fufferance.

Then wilt thou nere repent the of thy woe
But wifh it had been twentie folde as much
For *Iefus* fake, who euen in earth beloe
Can frollick thy incinder with his tutch
   And faire be-heauen thy bones in drearie graue,
   Aboue the glorie and eafe that *Cæfars* haue.

G 3

*A*nd

And footh to fay, wherin hath *Iefus* err'd
Or not deferu'd fuch fuffrance at thy hands?
*H*ath he not alwayes in his life preferr'd
Difgrace and dole to rid thee out of bands?
   Oh, was not he the man, the Lambe that dy'd
   To fhew thee heauen In woe, and not in pride?

He was Almightie to haue fau'd his head
If he had pleaf'd; But for a prefident
Of pafsiue Fortitude, and Lamblihead
He condifcended vnto woe and torment,
   And did erect the Croffe a capitall
   Enfigne of honour, and renowne to all.

And fince, what Saint did euer amount to bleffe
That hath not more or leffe been crucifi'd?
Either with felfe zeale-doome, or by oppreffe
Of tyrannie by villaines hands inflicted?
   The feed that muft to flowery growth redound
   Muft firft lie dead, and withered in the ground.

Befides; oh what a monftrous thing it is
To liue delirious vnder a thorney head;
Thy God to daigne to die for thy amiffe
And thou repine to be difhonored
   For Vertues fake; Oh fond ingratitude
   So to permit thy Sence thy Soule delude.

If

If ſo the fleſh, the world, the deuill could doe
More ſpight vnto thy ſtate then God can quayle,
Or that his grace could not tranſcend thy woe
Be-cheering it with happie counteruayle,
  Then might'ſt thou with a juſt repine deteſt
  To be by any fate of fleſh oppreſt.

But God both can and will relieue his Plaintife
That doth with juſt petitions inuoke him,
Selfe-loueleſſe and repineleſſe at the griefe
That from his foueraigne doome betides him ;
  The louing mothers teat is not ſo prone
  Vnto her Babe, as Chriſt to his deere one.

So ſhew'd his *Pellican* content to die
To giue thee life, the gore adowne his breaſt
To waſh away thy ſin-impuritie :
His dolour was thy euerlaſting reſt,
  His bitter wounds the euer open gates
  Of grace, and glorie to thy rankeſt fates.

Loe, he thy paines-appeaſe, true charter-warrant
Of glorie after gall : The bonnie bright
Whoſe crimſon rayes can faire propulſe and daunt
The dreadeſt Goblin of thy darkeſt night :
  Be thou the man of duty to thy dole,
  The reſt let him alone for to controle.

                                    Inſhrine

Inſhrine thy Patience in his Paſsion
Thy *H*ope, thy Conſtance in his after-boones
To his entire irradiation
Submit thy night-ſhades and decreaſed Moones,
 He is the Sonne of Right, and will appay
 All vertues anguor with a Hollie-day.

Behold his image yonder on the Croſſe,
See how he droops and dies and damnes Reuenge
Yeelding his whole humanity in groſſe
A pendular reproch on woodden henge :
 Yea euen his Deitie he doth dejeçt
 Vnto a feeming ſhadowed defeçt.

Be not a beaſt of deſperation,
A moodie torment, traitor to thy felfe,
T'is groſſe conceipt and imperfeçtion
To ground thy Barke vpon thy owne ſhores ſhelfe :
 Suffice it that extrinfecall aggriefe
 Abound, *fans* that thou giue it home-reliefe.

Thinke that thy finnes are greater then thy woe,
Thy worldly griefes but Graces happy refcue
From greater helles that to thy fowle doe growe ;
Or haply to enforce to manly vertue
 Thy youngling heſtes of grace ; or to containe
 Thy prefent good from proouing after vaine.
         Time

Time and thy graue did firft falute thy Nature
Euen in her infancie and cradle-Rightes
Inuiting it to duftie Deaths defeature,
*A*nd therewithall thy Fortunes fierce defpights :
   Death is the gulfe of all : and then I fay
   Thou art as good as *Cæfar* in his clay.

Death is the drearie Dad, and duft the Dame
Of all flefh-frailtie, woe or maieftie ;
All finkes to earth that furgeth from the fame,
Nature and Fortune muft together die :
   Only faire Vertue skales eternitie
   Aboue Earths all-abating tyrannie.

Read in my front the ruine of my nature
*A*nd therwithall perpend thy miferies,
I doe confeffe I were a curfed creature
Were not Gods grace aboue m'infirmities,
   So, thou in Faith to after-retribution
   *A*ffwage thy woe and tribulation.

Die in thy Sauiours wounds, and there an end,
There pricke the Period of thy moody wander,
To him thy woe, and the reuenge commend
As to thy foueraigne Liege and high commander.
   And thinke no errour whifpereth in thine eare
   For what I fay is true, and that I fweare.
               H   So

So faid : the teares of zeale trill'd downe his cheeks
Attefting truth vnto his Catechifme,
When (loe) eftfoons vnto the Crucifixe
Crooching adowne, he faid ; Oh facred Chrifme,
   Oh fweet affwage of infelicitie
   Witneffe that what I fay is veritie.

Say, art not thou the image of our Lord
The true Character of his fufferance ?
Was he not crown'd, deluded, and abhord
Mifuail'd, and fcourg'd with vile mif-valiance ?
   Oh, was not he the holie Pafchall lambe
   That di'd repineleffe for the finnes of man ?

Sweet (*Iefu*) giue me leaue to kiffe thy figure
With thankfull zeale to thy benignitie,
And let me pray thee by fo great diffigure
T'infpire this man of woe thy pafsiue-glorie :
   That not all like a beaft hee droop and die
   Heart-leffe and impious in his miferie.

Defend thy image from fo black a blurre
With thy in-fhine ; Let not temptation foyle
So much thy Pafsions price all like a Curre,
But as thou art a Prefident of toyle
   To after-glorie ; fo let thy grace fore-goe
   And faire accompanie this man of woe.

                            With

Without thy grace my fpeech is all but aire
And barraine Marle; it batteneth not the ground:
It is thy grace that foyfoneth all affaire
That holie grace which floweth from thy wound;
   I fpeak in flefh, inuefted in my bryer;
   There is no flame at all but from thy fire.

Make it appeare how good a God thou art
And how thy woundes were not in vaine inflicted,
What Nature cannot doe, let Grace impart
To ftrengthen and inhearten the afflicted,
   Shew that thy mercie is aboue the bound
   Of Fortunes topfie-turuie to confound.

Let not the fancies of a loftie ftile
And vaine mundanitie tranfport thy creature
As though alonlie Fortunes lowre or fmile
Were foueraigne Glories gift and dread defeature,
   As though thy power were worne out of date
   And could no longer figniorize our fate.

Difperfe the terrors of his moodie night
That he may fee thy fhone *Hierufalem*
And in this holie Cittie *Sions* light
Abide, and faithfullie beleeue this Theame
   Happie they all that fuffer for our Lord,
   For he to fuch his heauen will affoord.
H 2

With

With that he kiſt the Crucifixe againe
And with a ſtrict imbrace therof he founded ;
His Ghoſt amounted vp to heauens domaine,
*H*is corps lay trunke-like ſeeming dead confounded ;
 Whiles I meane while internallie infiered
 Did feele the woonders of Gods grace infpired.

Then gan I credit *Catechryſius*
*A*nd hatefullie abhor my former mood,
Baſe Melancholie, black and impious
That ſo diſtrayd me from eternall good :
 My heart exulted, and in zeale I ſwore,
 Now by our Lord, Ile be a beaſt no more.

I will no longer grudge at vertues toyle,
But gladly will be crucifi'd with *Ieſu* ;
No yron-fate ſhall heerafter foyle
My conſtancie vnto the Chriſt-croſſe rew :
 I will accompt all dollour and miſhap
 More deere then ſweeteſt Lullaby in Fortunes lap.

No longer will I wander vp and downe
The deſart of Reuenge, and dread Diſpaire,
But heer will ſtint me againſt miſ-fortunes frowne
A land-man of this ſoyle and happy aire :
 From hence I will reuiue to priſtin bleſſe
 Or els die heer with *Ieſu* in diſtreſſe.

          No

No fooner faid I fo, and gaue confent
To Graces in-come, and our Lords attaint,
But (loe) eftfoons from heauens high regiment
Muficke refounded, and appeaf'd my plaint.
   It was fo fweet aboue my feeble frayltie
   That downe I fell as one content to die.

Dying in fo fweet follace and in-heauen
I was no morē the man of earthly nature,
Gods Graces holie rellifh, and fweet leauen
Had altered my flefh to a new transfigure :
   Figure of zeale to be in I*e/us* armes,
   Condition to endure ten thoufand harmes.

But God who faw & wrought this alteration,
Faire interdicted Death his date-moft deed,
*A*nd fent an Angell from his holie region
To cheere my frailty vp to future fpeed :
   Whome when I faw and fmelt his heauenly hue,
   It did eftfoons my death to life renue.

He then out-ftepping from his filuer-cloud
Made toward me with a reuerend peacefull pace,
And as he march'd euer and anon he bow'd
Vnto the Crucifixe was there in place.
   Whereto at laft downe humbled, he kift it,
   And gaue it me in hand, and thus infpeecht it.

H 3

Hold

Hold heer (*Elizian*-man) thy Sauiours image
The typick *T*rophee of thy foules redeeme,
Be it thy lifes eternall *A*ppennage
Thy hearts deere daintie, and thy choice-efteeme,
   Inconfcience it within thy in-moft heft
   For *In hoc figno vinces* is expreft.

Be it thy Standard againft all affrount,
Vnder her fhade tire out Mif-fortunes weather,
Be true to it, and make a fure account
Heauen is thine owne as fure as God liues euer :
   God liues for euer to protect and pay
   His Champion with a ioy-eternall day.

*A*nd hether I come, fent from his Tabernacle
To certifie fo much to thy poor frailtie,
And heer haue brought thee heauen-inchanted tackle
To warfare flefh and bloods calamitie :
   Loe I thy *A*ngell of protection
   Againft whatfoere foule and fell affection.

With that he arm'd my Head with Reafons Helme,
The Creft was Vigilance ; the Plumes were twaine
Temprance againft faire Fortunes ouerwhelme,
And Patience againft her angrie vaine :
   The Gorget was Content, and either Pouldron
   Was humble Prayer and Meditation.

                                 The

The Corſlet, it was Zeale of Gods true honour,
The Back peece, Hope to after-retribution,
The Gauntlets, tackles to Charities endeuour,
The Vant-braces, Faiths decke and decoration,
  The Martch, he did injoyne was Penitence,
  The Combate, Courage againſt all ſinnes offence.

Then gaue he me in hand a Shield of Golde
All ouer-grauen with Chriſtes Paſsion,
And round about in-amill'd I might behold
Death-heads, and latter Reſurrection
  To heauen or hell: The Croſſe in th'other hand
  Was all my Spear againſt whatſoerc withſtand.

Thus arm'd; the *A*ngell bright againe in-clouded
Vpbounded from mine eye toward heauen away
Leauing the place with ſpiced ſweetes ſuffuſed
And all beſtrew'd with Crownes and wreathes of Bay,
  Spelles and demonſtrances of ſuture glorie
  To well atchiued warre and victorie.

I then there all alone vn-Angelled,
Began to view and glee me in mine Armes
Woondring to ſee me ſo be-Championed
*A*gainſt th'aſſaults of ſin and Fortunes harmes:
  And thus I ſaid: Oh ſhone *Hieruſalem*
  What woonders are in thee to well-fare men.

I bleffe the God and Spirit of thy bounds,
I bleffe thy Concord and thy Monarchie,
I bleffe the ftreams that tril from *Iefus* wounds
Into thy feuen-fold Cefternes ; and from thee
   *A*re vitally imparted vnto all
   That liue within thy Rampier and thy wall.

Loe, I with Graces furniture faire arm'd
Within thy confines, humbly befeech thee
Admit my Souldiour-fhip as yet vn-harm'd
With any aduerfe warres, into thy cittie :
   And daigne me there a ftand againft all euill,
   The flefh, the world, and fierce infulting deuill.

In thee I fee how much I went amiffe
Ranging the defart of mundanitie,
And in thy wifedom nowe I learne this
That not in Fortunes falfe malignitie
   But in finnes guilt, and grimme captiuitie
   Is only wracke, and blacke calamitie.

I fee my miffe in thy faire Phifnomie,
My way-leffe errours in thy vnitie,
I feele the ardure of true Chiualrie
Infpired in me from thy Nobility :
   Heere liue I then the remnant of my age
   Vnder thy haughty woorth and Patronage.

                    So

So faid ; a filuer bell from high refounded
Sommoning that Region round about to facring,
When (loe) eftfoons *Catechryfius* vn-fwounded
His foules returne did giue him new reuiuing,
  Oh facred fommon, fweet enchanting peale
  That fo from heauen to earth couldft foules repeale.

*H*is face like *Phæbus* in his Noony-fhine
Daunted my feeble eye at prime afpect,
His foules regreffe had made it fo diuine,
Bebrightning cleane away all fraile defect,
  As had not zeale inheartened my frayltie,
  I had not had the power t'abide fuch glorie.

He then vp-rifing toward me aduanced
And kift the Crucifix I had in hand,
So done ; he faid : Sweet *Iefu* be thou thanked
That haft vouchfau'd my prayer to vnderftand ;
  Confirme him in thy grace for now and euer
  That from thy loue and laud he varie neuer.

With that he imbrac'd me with a frount of glee
*A*nd call'd me brother, and Coparcener
Of *Chriftes* Domaine, and therwithall he gaue me
A golden ring ; the poefie was *Perfeuer* :
  So, foorth we went vnto the Temple-ward
  Twas facring time, and mufick much we heard.

      I   Along

Along as vp the Rocke we footed it
He did congratulate my fhone in armor
And did expound vnto me euery whit
*H*ow I might vfe it to Gods greateft honor
   *A*nd then concluded: O *Elizian*
   See what it is to be a Chriftian.

Wouldft thou haue thought in thy mundanitie
That euer Fortunes heel had had the might
To fpurne th' away to fuch an after-glorie?
Or that thy forie iourneyment all night
   Would euer haue brought thee to fweet repofe
   As now thou feeleft farre aboue thy woes?

The ball out-banded from the court of game,
Fals not of force into the durtie kennell,
But marke, and often fhalt thou fee the fame
Flie in at Pallace-windowes, and there reuell
   Vpon the royal Mattes, and rich embroader;
   Such grace of God hath blowne thy frailtie hether.

Not all the flufh of thy fore-frollicke ftate,
The worfhip of thy birth, thy rich reuenue,
Thy countries high applaud and eftimate
*A*nd all that faire E*lyzium* can yeeld youe,
   Is of the worth to countervayle thys hap
   Fallen from faire Fortune into Graces lap.

                               Say

Say that E*liza* is the Lords deere daintie,
The *Phænix* of true *P*rincipalitie
The feaſt of peace and ſweet ſaturitie
Vnto the people of her Emperie;
   Say that ſhe is both Grace and Natures none-ſuch
   I bend my knee; and ſay and thinke as much.

For I haue heard the woonders of her name
Our coaſts is full of great E*lizabeth,*
Yea, all the world is fertill of the fame;
Sweet Name that all mens pennes and tongues inableth,
   *S*weet Sound that all mens ſences lullabieth,
   Sweet Marle that all the world imbatteneth.

But ſuch her glories are but eare-delightes
*A*nd lip-ſweets only to our far awayes,
For we are no E*lizium*-bred wightes
Nor haue we any ſuch like merrie dayes;
   Wee haue our joyes in another kind
   Ghoſtly innated in our foule and mind.

Whom angour of miſhap or guilt of ill
Driues to diſpaire, and ſelfe miſdoomfull deed,
Loe, heer th'vnfraught of his woe-loaden will
And reuerend riches to his ghoſtly need;
   Loe, heer his Arke againſt the inundation
   Of Sinne and Fortunes funerall-temptation.

I 2

Heer

*H*eer (loe) the amitie of men and Angels
In uniforme adore of one true God,
Heer *P*eace and Pietie togither dwels,
Heer Scifme, and Difcords clouen-foot nere trod,
   Heer facred Ceremonies are in vre
   *A*s wedlocke-rightes twixt Faith and Soules infure.

*H*eer chantes the Nightingale incefsant praife
And prayer vnto the Orient fonne of God,
Heer Grace our vncouth Adamifme allayes
*S*tepping her golden foot wher guilt erft trod,
   Heer *S*acrifice and Sacrificer both
   Gods bleffe and good acceptance ftill fore-goeth.

He would haue told me more to this pourport,
But that his vp-hill pace out-tyr'd his fpeech
*A*nd now were alfo neer the Temple port
Where euerie fight I faw was fo heauenly rich
   As had he vttered more mine eies delight
   Had quite vndone mine eares to doe him right.

Ah, now I want the Mufe of *Salomon*
To tell you a Temple-tale, a tale of truth
*A*ll of the Architeɛt and frame of *Sion* :
To tell you of her age and of her youth
   And of her reuerend raigne and regiment
   *A*nd how *Doble∬a* rues her high achiuement.

                        The

The grownd was Faith ; the meane worke Charitie
The Top, a Hopefull apprehenſion
Of heauens attaine : All was of Vnitie
A ſollid mettle heawn out of Chriſt his Paſsion :
   Yea Chriſt himſelfe was fundamentall ſtone,
   And all the Sowder was Deuotion.

There ſhin'd the Rubie and the Chryſolite
The ſparkling Diamond, and the Emeraud greene,
Each Saphyre in their ſeuerall delight :
There was the happie Iacent to be ſeene
   The Topaſſe, Onyx, and many a faire gem,
   Corrall, Amber, and Aggats were traſh among thẽ.

Which ſuch bright rough-caſt ouer all incruſted
T'was heauen to ſee what Rain-bowe rayes it yeelded
Whiles euerie gem ambitiouſly contended
T'out-ſtare each others ſtarry neighbourhed :
   It was ynough t'illumine all the world
   But for the myſts that falſe *Dobleſſa* hurld.

Roſes and flowers of all cullored kindes,
The Marie-buſh and pleaſant Eglantine
The Honey-ſuckle in her twiſted twines
Immixt with Yuie, and the Grape-full Vine,
   Did all growe vp that ſtarrie ſpanglement
   Spouſing her ſplendure with their ſpiced ſent.

I 3

Below

Below thefe heauen-amounting fwauities
Grew ouer all the Temple-greene befide
Sweet Gilliflowers and Primrofes
The Pink, and Gerifole (the Suns deer bride ;)
    The Molie, Violet, and the pleafant Dafie
    Balme, Margerum, and fweet Coaft-marie.

There grew the loftie Cedar, and the Pine,
The peacefull Oliffe, and the martiall Firre
The verdant Laurell in her fhadie-fhine,
The patient Palme, and penitentiall Mirrhe :
    The Elme, the Poplar, and the Cipreffe tree
    And all trees els that pleafant are to fee.

All kinds of fruits were there perpetuall
The Date, the Almond, & the fauceful Citron,
The Fig, the Orange, and Pomegranet royall,
The Quince, the Abricock, and the musk-Mellon
    The Plumme, the Cherie, and the pleafant Peare
    The Filberd and the Mulberie grew there.

Amid thefe trees, thefe fruits, thefe flowerie fweetes
Ran in a Maze-like wile a chryftall ftreame
Of heauenly Nectar ; in whofe fweet floods and fleets
Swom fholes of fifhes, euerie fifhes gleame
    Brighter than *Tytan* in his Southerne ftage :
    This ftreame was ftrong againft prime guiltes enrage.

                                                    Her

*H*er filent murmur was fo muficall
As it diffolu'd the Rock to fand and grauell
Whereby it might more in efpeciall
With multiplicitie of eares incell
 Her mufick-fweets : yea euen the earth beloe
 Did open, and eruct her bowels therto.

There fate the Mauis and the Nightingale
Carrolling their Layes vnto th'eternall fpring
The little Larke high houering ouer all :
There euery bird did either play or fing,
 The Parrat for his plumes did moft excell
 But Phænix bare away the triumph-bell.

There was no fauage fhape, no Laruall hue
No Bug, no bale, no horrid Owlerie
But all that there was, was fincere and true,
Her fweets, her fpendure, & her mufick-glee ;
 Yea euen the Angels of Diuinitie
 Were of that league, and Confraternitie.

Whiles thus with facred follace I furuayd
The Temples outward majeftie, and heauen,
So long on that imparadize I ftayd
That now the Temple clocke did ftrike eleuen :
 It was the inftant time of high Oblation
 We might no longer linger, but begon.

       Eftfoons

Eftfoons we did fo pace-fullie aduance
That to the Temple-dore we ftraight arriu'd,
Ore which was grauen, *Vna*, M*ilitans*
Aftile from Vnitie, and Warre deriu'd ;
  The gate was all of pure beaten golde,
  The Portch a funnie Zodiacke to behold.

Then in we entred, (oh, we entred in)
Pleafe God I neuer may come foorth againe :
What faw I there ? Oh my eyes were dimme
My foule, my fubftance all was poore and vaine
  To comprehend fo high magnificence ;
  Yet what I can I will you it difpence.

I Spanield after *Catechryfius* foot
A happie fhaddow to good a fubftance :
All like a flower as yet but in thee root
*T*ending to future growth, and fhone aduance :
  The Temple-porter was a reuerend man
  And was t'admit in no *Elizian.*

Then ask'd he *Catechryfius* who I was
Who anfwered a *Catecumen* hee,
With that he greeted me, and let me paffe,
Such was my entrie to felicitie :
  The Temple gates were fower and this was it
  Which none but *Europe*-fpirits might admit.

                          There

There on my knees my heart was full of fire,
Fire of the grace of God (deere grace of God)
Which ſtrong bemettled my zeales aſpire
To view the glorie of that ſhone abod :
  It was a Pigion from the Temple-top
  Which all that frame, and glorie did vp prop.

A Pigeon whiter then the whiteſt Pigion
Solie ſubſiſtant of his owne pure E*ſſe*,
His *Poſſe* was Sanctification,
And Graces bounteous liberalitie ;
  What *Ieſus* erſt had planted with his blood
  This Pigion gaue it grace-full liuelihood.

The beames which iſſued from his brightſome briſt
Were ſuch as none but *Sion* euer ſaw
Nor euer could *Dobleſſas* dreary miſt
Indarken, or reſemble, or withdraw ;
  Loue, Peace, and Magnanimity in good
  Patience, and Prudence aboue all fleſh and blood.

Iuſtice, and Temperance, and Benignitie,
Zeale, and internall Conſolation,
Pittie, and hopefull Longanimitie,
Obedience, and brotherly Correction,
  Deuotion, and Mortification
  *A*nd firme affiance in our Lords Saluation. · · · ·

K

Such

Such were the Pigions rayes from Temple-top
Which like a heauen of light illumin'd all,
It being therto a more fecure vpprop
Then any lime and ftone, or brafen wall :
  Oh S*ion*, S*ion* happie Cittie thow
  So holie-ghofted againft all ouerthrow.

Then looking downe vnto the refidue
I might difcerne a reuerend minifterie
Of men and Angels chanting vnto *Iefu*
Inceffant Hymnes of praife and Iubilie ;
  The high Sacrificator at the *A*ltar
  Victiming with holie rites his makar.

What fhall I fay of all the maieftie
Of all the reuerend rites and ceremonies
The rich adorne, the heauenly melodie,
The lufter, and the precious fwauities
  *T*hat there I faw, felt, heard, and vnderftood ?
  Oh, they tranfcended farr poore flefh and blood.

For, what the goodneffe and the power of God
In their immenfitie could jointlie doe
Was there in force *fans* bound or period,
His grace and glory both did tend therto :
  The meaneft obiect there vnto my fence
  Was more then all the worlds magnificence.

There

There faw I facred impofition
Of hands; and grace abundantly imparted,
Chrifme, and autentique Sanctification
And Exorcifme of fuch as were poffeffed:
    Their credence and their language was alike
    All *Babell*-Biblers they did dead diflike.

There was no fcambling for the Ghofpels bread
But what a publike Vnitie diliured
The fame a prompt Credulitie receiued;
Their humbleneffe was fo beholie-ghofted
    As Pride had not the power to entice
    The wifeft of them all to a new deuice.

Cafting my eye afide, I might difcrie
Selected troopes of people from the reft
Dooming themfelues with great aufteritie
Both men and women in difcullored veft;
    They were the people of vowes, and high afpire
    Endu'd with Graces more efpeciall fire.

On no hand could I caft my liquorifh eie
From heauenlie miracles and myfteries;
Some fchool'd their Pupils fraile infirmitie
Difpencing them Gods facramentall graces,
    Some raif'd the dead, and fome expulft the deuill,
    Yet nought could make *Doblefsa* fee her euill.

K 2

How

How manie *S*ionits of choife eftceme
Braue men of woonders haue beene fent from thence
To teach D*obleſſa* (Errors dreary Queene)
Their Temples fanctimonie and innocence?
 How many worthies haue difpenft their blood
 To doe th' vnkind D*obleſsa* fo much good.

But fhe, oh fhe accurfed Sorcereffe
Would neuer yet belecue, nor grce their grace
But ftill perfifteth in her wretchedneffe
Warfaring with bloody broile this happy place;
 Yea, had fhe might according to her malice
 S*ion* had been a ruine long ere this.

She was a Witch, and Queen of all the Defert
From *Babell*-mount vnto the pit of *H*ell,
She forc'd nor God, nor any good defert,
She could doe any thing faue doing well:
 Her law was Libertie, her luft was Pride
 And all good awe and order fhe defi'd.

Erft ere this Temple was eftablifhed
She had no being at all aboue the earth
But euer lay in dcepeft hell abyffed;
Why did not God confound her in her birth?
 Oh, t'was becaufe his Temple might attaine
 Through her affaults to be more foueraigne.

Gods

Gods Lambe was now both bred and dead out-right
To ranfome all the world from finnes inthrall,
And to fecure it in more happie plight
Had built this Sanctuarie facramentall.
   It fhin'd fo fhone vnto Gentilitie
   That it began to fee, and gree her glorie.

And as the merrie riuer to the Maine
Or the in-ayred ftone downe to his Center
Fleets and defcends as to their due domaine,
So it to Sion confluently bent her:
   Yea, had this hag not been fo timely bred
   The world had all ere this been Sioned.

For fhe could quaintly maske in Sions guize
And fucke out venym from the Flower of life,
And fo retayle it with her fubtilties
For pureft honey: Such was her deed of ftrife;
   Her woluifh nature in a lamblie hue
   Shee could difguize, and feeme of Sions crue.

Like Enfignes fhe oppof'd to Sions Enfignes,
Like her pretence of grace, and Gods high honor,
Like Grapes fhe did contend grew vp her Vines,
And as good Gold as Sions feem'd her Coppor;
   It was but feeming fo, not fo indeed,
   Her feeming-flower was a very weed.

K 3

For

For why, the ſpirit which ſhe did pretend
Was not autentique from the holy Ghoſt,
On no authority ſhe did depend
Nor had ſhe certaine being in any coaſt ;
　　Her owne beheſt ſhe did Idolatrize,
　　And *Hydra*-like renu'd her Fallacies.

She had no Altar, nor no Sacrament
No Ceremonie, nor Oblation,
Her ſchool was Cauill, & truthleſſe babblement
Riot her Raigne, her end damnation ;
　　This was the haggard whoore of *Babylon*
　　Whoſe cup inuenym'd all that drunke thereon.

And this was ſhe which now this holie-day
Whiles all the Temple was in deep deuotions
*A*nd high adore of Chriſts natiuity
Came with her barbarous Babellonians
　　To bid it battell, and aſſault the place ;
　　But (oh the foole) ſhe came againſt Gods grace.

She came with peace-full Oliffe in her hand
Pretending mutuall honour of that feaſt :
And all her rabble-rout ſhe did command
As much in outward fayning to proteſt,
　　But vnderneath their plauſible attire
　　They all bare balles of venym and wild-fire.

　　　　　　　　　　　　　　　　　　　She

She was more craftie then Gentilitie
Which thought of yore with maſſacre to quell
The propagation of Sionrie :
For well ſhe wiſt that *Sion* was as a bell
  And Perſecution but as a clapper
  That made her ſiluer-ſound more far to ſcatter.

Shee therfore to beguile with friendlie ſeeming
Came thus addreſt ; and priuily intempled
Her ſpeciall *Bout-fieux* to prepare her comming
With ſeeds and weeds of jealoſie and falſhed :
  Meane while ſhe ſtood without the Temple gate
  Proteſting zeale and dutie to her ſtate.

But God whoſe ſpirit euer *Argus*-ey'd
The weale of *Sion* as th'apple of his eye,
Saw from his high enthrone, and did deride
The Harlots complot ; and did by and by·
  Inſpire his Templers pregnant jealoſie
  And valure againſt her ſlie hoſtilitie.

Efts might you heare a battle-bell peale out
Religious Larums ouer all the Region
And ſee a ſolempne confluence about
The high Sacrificators holie Oblation :
  Each one was on his knees for Confirmation
  In grace againſt ſo vile prevarication.

                      Amongſt

*A*mongſt the reſt was I a *Catecumen*
As yet vngrac'd with his alhallowed hand,
Vntil ſuch time as *Catechryſius* then
Preſented me, and gaue him t'vnderſtand
  My Name, my Nation, and Conuerſion
  And how I crau'd to be a man of *Sion*.

*T*hen tooke he mee by the hand, and did applaud
Such my *Primitiæ* toward ſo high reſolue,
Bleſsing my on-gate fram *Doblessas* fraud
And ſanctifying me with a holie ſalue ;
  He wept for joy that an E*lizian*
  Would come to be his Metropolitan.

*A*nd for he ſaw me abſolutely arm'd
Alreadie to the warres ; he ſaid no more
But only bleſt me, and with his breath becharm'd
My Conſtancie againſt the *Babell*-whore :
  And for I was an E*ngliſh*-Ilander
  He prickt me downe vnder Saint *Georges* banner.

Then C*atechryſius* tooke me by the hand
And led me to my Cullors ; and as we went
He briefly told me and gaue me t'vnderſtand
How all *Dobleſsas* dorrs I might preuent,
  *A*nd then concluded. Oh, that E*liza* were
  A Sionite to day to ſee this geere.

                              By

By this *Doblefsa* feeing all her guile
Detected and Alarum'd ouer all,
Was in a pelting chafe, and gan reuile
The name of *Sion*, and to fcale the wall :
   Loe, thus began the holie warres of *Sion*
   Againft the rampant Hagg and whoore of *Babylon*.

Then might you fee whole Legions of Angels
Difcend adowne in amitie of warre
To Sion, againft *Doblessa* and her deuels :
The warre was like as when proud *Lucifar*
   Tumulting all the Court of heauen was throwne
   He, and his complices to hell adowne.

Eftfoones the high *S*acrificator feeing
The vp-fhot brunt of all *Doblessas* broyle
Came perfonally himfelfe vnto the bickering
To cheere his men of warre in all their toyle :
   *A*nd thus befpake them from the holie Tower,
   His fpeech and geft was full of grace and power.

Oh men of *Sion*, happy Machabies,
Whom Temples honor in your foules ingrafted
*H*ighlie demeanes to Gods benignities ;
Difmay not at the number of the dead
   But thinking who he is for whom you fight
   Redouble your proweffe, and your manly might.
             L   You

You combate for the high H*ierufalem*
A region of Peace and Immortalitie
Fore-fpell'd, and promift only vnto them
That ftraine in her behalfe their vp-fhot conftancie :
   Nor feare yee any woundes or any dying
   So good a death tends to a better reuiuing.

See, how confufedly D*oblefsa* fightes
Without all difcipline or good array,
Her Camp abandon'd to inteftine fpightes
And euerie one contending to beare fway ;
   Their owne diforder will confound their power
   The frame of Difcord dures not an hower.

On then like gallants of the holy-Ghoft
Fighting in Vnity, and for a Crowne
Againft a rafcall and tumultuous Hoft ;
Nere let the ftrumpet pull the Temple downe,
   No, neuer fhall the ftrumpet pull it downe
   For God is God, and it is all his owne.

Rememorate the glorie of her Age,
And of her Raigne, and of her priftin Warres
How often hath fhe quell'd D*oblefsas* rage
Attempting to affayle her holy Rampiars ?
   Hath fhe not been a Nurfe vnto yee all
   A Shelter, and a feaft moft feftiuall ?

                          Befides

Befides, hath God not promifed of yore
That hell fhall nere preuaile againft her gates ?
And hath not he vouchfau'd to die therfore
Eftablifhing her glorie againft all Fates ?
 Yea, is not he her fundamentall ftone
 Her daylie Sacrifice and high Oblation ?

What will ye more ? Oh Sionities no more,
But to your tacklings ftand like men of honor
Like men of *Sion*, one to twentie fcore
Such *Babell*-hildings ; mortifie their rancor
 With conftant and imperious refiftance,
 God and his Angels are in your afsiftance.

So faid, he bleft them, and difmift them all ;
Who ftraight in troops vnto the Rampiers ran
And happie he could get vpon the wall :
There then a fecond skirmifh frefh began,
 Dobleſſa ftill perfifting in th'affault
 And *Sion* fierce fupplying all default.

It was a heauen to fee the good array
And vnitie of *Sion* in this conflict,
How euerie one was willing to obay
His Officers encharge though nere fo ftrict,
 The holy-Ghoft was in and ouer all
 Cheering their combate with his cordiall.

L 2

Meane

Meane while the high Sacrificator, he
Attended to the Temples Sacrifice
Offring it vp for peace and victorie,
He chanted *H*ymnes, and Laudes, and Letanies,
   And in Pontificall Procefsion
   He and his Clergie made their intercefsion.

Some in their ftuddies commented the Text
Conferring place with place, and with traditions
Ov'ring the fraud wherwith *Doblessa* vext
Their Ghofpels peace ; fome others in her ftations
   Boldlie aduentured their liues to tell
   The Babellonians of all her hell.

Some they perfwaded, thofe were verie few
*A*nd of thofe few not one of ten perfifted,
But ftill as fear and fraud their frailties drew
They ftarted backe againe like men agafted :
   Oh, what it is to be too fecular,
   It was felf-loue that all their weale did marre.

And of fuch braue aduenturous Sionites
As *Doblessa* could by hooke or crooke intrap
They di'd the death, and fuffred all the fpights
That rage and rafcall wit could jointly rap,
   Subject they were to dreadfull perfecution
   By publick edict, and falfe brethrens treafon.

                       What

What facring, and what facramenting was
In *Sion* all this while for *Sions* fafetie
Was more then all the ftrength of ftone and braffe
In her defence ; God not in enmitie
   But for her greater glories fake permitting
   Dobleffa thus to bid it bale and bickring.

Contrarie-wife, *Dobleffa* ru'd the fate
Of her attempt ; her mood began to quaile,
For God now feeing the prefixed date
Of *Sions* patience in her laft auayle
   Did on the fuddaine fo enlarge his grace
   That th'whoore retir'd, and gaue backe apace.

*A*nd then to fhew her lateft trumperie
(Now that our Lords permifsion faild her powre)
She gan with Magick-fpels and forcerie
Faire Virgin-like to falfifie her figure,
   Therby to feeme as gracious as fhe could
   To *Sions* eie ; fuch was her guize of ould.

But when fhe faw that all her fallaces
And fierce affaults to *Sion* were in vaine,
And feeling now withall Gods heauie furies
Showre down vpon her like a floud of raine,
   Shee could no longer bide the brunt of *Sion*
   But backe fhe reel'd to hell and *Babylon.*

L 3

And

And fearing leaft her daunted enterprize
Might haplie alien her peoples hearts
From her obeyance: She fo bewitcht their eies
With myftes of falfed glory, and high deferts,
   That they befotted in their difafter
   Betooke them to their heeles, and fled with her.

And as they fled, Oh, marke their vanitie,
They did fo crauin-cockadoodle it
*A*s though they had run away victorie
And left faire S*ion* in her dying fit,
   Such hoopes, fuch clangor, and fuch fymphonie
   And all was but D*obleſſas* pollicie.

She nufled them in fo proud Peacockrie
To th' end they might not fee their damned ftate,
But ftill perfeuer as the Bumble-Bee
Repine-leffe in their dung, and defperate:
   Oh, curfed and vnkind captiuitie
   To be fo willing drudge to Falfitie.

Yet fome whome S*ions* more efpeciall beame
Had bright appaid to fee her dignitie
Fled from the witch, as wak'd from out a dreame
Of Faery, and Chimericall Imagerie,
   Such S*ion* intromitted in her gate
   Applauding them with deere congratulatc.

                              Contrary

Contrarie-wife whatfoeuer Sionite
Dobleſſa could with flight or fight enthrall
She led away into eternall night
Blind-folding their eyes to make them fall
    Into a thoufand helles and offendickles,
    Thrife fatall lapfe from Grace into fuch pickles.

Nor was the holie Temple thus acquitted
For euer after from her hoftill trouble
But ftill as *Hydra*-like fhe had renued
One head vpon the others ftump and ftubble
    She came againe, and made a braggard-fhow,
    But ftill fhe bare away the Palfie-blow.

Such being the ancient league of God to *Sion*
Necefsiting her Peace to fuch temptation
And yet withall protefting his protection
Therto : againft all hell and *Babylon* :
    What greater fafetie then fo good affurance ?
    The word of God is of eternall durance.

Thus *Sion* triumpht ouer moode and tumult
Cabaging her Peace in perfect vnitie
Againft whatfoeuer future-Scifmes infult :
And feeing now no more hoftilitie
    But all the Regions cleere : She fell a rifling
    Dobleſſas fpoyles, the Honors of her fighting.

                    And

And in her warlike wardrop there ſhe plaſt them
Amongſt a world of former pillages
And ſpoyles of *Babell*: high H*ieruſalem*
Siſterlie applauding ſuch her victories,
　And thinking long the day to honor her
　With her embrace, and euerlaſting cheere.

Then (to conclude) the high Sacrificator
Came foorth in place, and bleſt the Combatants,
Bidding them giue to God th' eternall honour
Of ſo high hap: And therupon he deſcants
　A large diſcourſe of Gods protection
　How prompt he alwayes was to ſuccour S*ion*.

So done: he efts diſmiſt the multitude
T' attend vnto the buriall of their brethren
Whom S*ions* honor had that day endu'd
With zeale to die for her like valiant men ;
　Their graues reſented Immortalitie
　Sweeter then all the ſents of *Arabie*.

And for it was a ſpeciall victorie
*A*tchiu'd euen on the very walles of S*ion,*
There was proclaim'd a generall Iubilie
To be follemniz'd throughout all the region
　The Octave after ; in feaſt-full reference
　*A*nd thanks to God for ſuch his high defence.

　　　　　　　　　　　　　　　　　　　In

In which meane while the holie Sacrificer
Progreſsing the Prouince, viſited his flocke
And with his paſtorall care, and Crozier
Out-weeded and retrenched from the ſtocke
    Whatſoeuer venym weed, or graft of Error
    Dobleſſa had ſowne, or ſet with guile, or terror.

Namelie; he did eſpecially diſpoſe
To carefull cure the wownded Combatantes;
And ſuch as brunt of warre had ſlaine; all thoſe
H'Incallendred to Fames rememberance :
    Laſtly, he did repaire and fortifie
    Each ruine againſt all future enemie.

By this the Octave-day of victorie
Was come, when (loe) the Temples ſiluer belles
Safely out-pealed to feſtivitie ;
Then might you ſee both Sionits and Angels
    Troop to the Temple-ward like ſwarmes of Bees
    And hand in hand downe falling on their knees.

You may imagine, no ; you are to fraile
To comprehend ſo high magnificence :
There ſawe I heauen and earth in ioynt-entayle
Homaging to Gods beneuolence
    A world of praiſe and Alleluyaes,
    Hallowing the aire with ſo thankfull praiſe.
                M

I faw the high Procefsion paffe along
In intermixed rankes of men and Angels
The holie-Ghoft ouer-hov'ring their fong:
There founded Mufic-inftruments and Belles;
    Yea, birds conforted with their warbling lays,
    T' enter-common alfo in this dayes praife.

Along as thus we march'd about the Temple
In rich array, in fweetes, and mellodie,
A fuddaine Zephire-gale blew from the ftceple
Solliciting our eyes fupernally,
    And what it was; Oh, there I bend my knee
    It was a Virgin in bright maieftie.

The skie did open, and adowne difcended
Vpon a filuer-cloud this follempne fight
A Mayden-Nymph moft fhone-fatellited
With all the Angell-court of heauen out-right:
    She was inuefted in as Orient fplender
    As Gods omnipotence and Loue could lend her.

She was the *Genium* of high *Hierufalem*
The Patroneffe of S*ion*, and the Aduocate
Of grace and mercie vnto mortall men;
Her coming was for to congratulate
    This triumph-day and gratefull Iubilie
    Of S*ion* vnto God for victorie.

Which

Which fuch her prefence ftinted our Procefsion
Rapting vs all into a fweet admire
Of fo fhone figure ; her irradiation
Flaming our fpirits with a mightie fire
   Of Seraphin-affeçtion and zeale
   To die in vifion of her fweet reueale.

I may not be fo impious and prophane
*A*s to compare this heauenly fpeçtacle
To any earthlie pomp or jollie vaine
Of *Cæfars* Bride : whofe pride is but a cackle
   Or as a fhadow in comparifon
   Of fo triumphant and moft virgin vifion.

There on the Temple-pinacle fhe refted
Gracing, and doubling our follempne feaft
With her in-heauen ; And all the while fhe attefted
Both with her glee-full countenance and geft
   Gods euerlafting loue vnto the place
   And eke her owne againft *Dobleffas* race.

At laft fhe gan to waue and wend about
Our follempne multitude with all her traine
Sufpending vs in a delitious doubt
Of fome fweet fequell : Our doubt was not in vaine,
   For on the fuddaine houering ouer vs
   She fhowr'd downe Rofes moft odoriferous.

Rofes

Rofes both red and white adowne fhe fhewred
From out her virgin-lap, fo fweet refenting
As all our fences into fent adiured :
So done ; fhe vanifht, leauing vs a fcambling
　　For fuch her fweets ; I for my part was one
　　That neuer would giue ouer till all had done.

And ftill I call'd vpon E*lizas* name
Thinking thofe Rofes hers, that figure hers,
Vntill fuch time as *Catechryfius* came
And pointing me vnto his faithfull teares
　　(Teares of the zeale he bare t' *Elizas* name)
　　He told me No ; fhe was an Efterne Dame.

With that I caft mine eye into the Eaft
Where yet I might difcerne the region bright,
Much like as when the Sunne downe in the Weft
Newly difcended, leaues vs of his light
　　Some Rubie-Rellickes after : Oh, deer God
　　Why made fhe not with vs more long abod.

Rapt with thefe woonders, wrapt in virgin-Rofes
*A*nd faire be-Sioned againft misfortune,
I fuddainly was gone from thefe repofes
Sollicited with an efpeciall importune
　　Of home-ward zeale and of E*lizas* name,
　　Wherto I bend, and fay ; God bleffe the fame.

FINIS.

CPSIA information can be obtained
at www.ICGtesting.com
Printed in the USA
LVHW081006040219
606292LV00003B/377/P